THE POWER OF FAITH FILLED WORDS

HOW TO STOP NEGATIVE SELF-TALK AND GET WHAT YOU SAY

FRANCIS K.D. JONAH

TABLE OF CONTENT

INTRODUCTION........3

CHAPTER ONE: WORDS CREATE THINGS......8

CHAPTER TWO: WORDS DETERMINE YOUR DIRECTION IN LIFE......9

CHAPTER THREE: WORDS MIXED WITH FAITH WORK, NOT IDLE WORDS.........11

CHAPTER FOUR: KNOW WHO YOU ARE TO BE FREE FROM NEGATIVE SELF TALK.........13

CHAPTER FIVE: SPEAK A NEW LANGUAGE..........14

COPYRIGHT

No part of this book should be used without the express written permission of the author

SCRIPTURES

All scriptures are taken from the King James Version of the Bible, unless otherwise stated

INTRODUCTION

Imagine living in a world where everything you say comes to pass.

Imagine asking trees to die and they die instantly.

Imagine asking the dead to rise and they rise instantly.

Imagine asking sickness to go and it goes instantly.

Imagine asking your business to flourish and it flourishes.

Imagine asking your finances to improve and it improves.

Now! Stop imagining. All these can be a reality if you deliver yourself from negative self-talk and learn how to use the power of faith filled words.

Idle words will not produce the results we want.

Join me in this journey to cause exploits with our words.

IMPORTANT

My name is Francis Jonah. I believe all things are possible. It is because of this belief that I have achieved so much in life. This belief extends to all. I believe every human being is equipped to succeed in every circumstance, regardless of the circumstance.

I know the only gap that exists between you and what you need to achieve or overcome is knowledge.

People are destroyed for lack of knowledge.

It is for this reason that I write short practical books that are so simple, people begin to experience immediate results as evidenced by the many testimonies I receive on daily basis for my various books.

This book is no exception. You will obtain results because of it.

GET 4 POWERFUL FREE BOOKS
Click Here To Get the Books Below in Your Email

Click Here to Get them Now

The Four Powerful Books are:
1. **All Things Are Possible**
2. **Power of I Am**
3. **Power of Praise**
4. **Power of Positive thinking**

Click Here to Get them Now

Counselling Or Prayer

Send me an email if you need prayer or counsel or you have a question.

Better still if you want to make my acquaintance
My email is drfrancisjonah@gmail.com

CHAPTER ONE: WORDS CREATE THINGS

The world was created by words.
The tool that God employed to create the whole world was words.
In the same way our mouths have creative power.
Death and life are in the power of our tongue.
We eat the fruits of our lips.
The words we speak are seeds; they will produce harvests in our lives.
It is the reason we must be careful of what we say.
Some people use words to insult and curse. They use words to call themselves losers.
The say things like "nothing good can come out of me".
Why would you use the very powerful tool of creation to destroy your own life?
We need to rethink our use of words.
Words have creative power.
When you speak, healing can happen, things can die, things can flourish.
Actually anything can happen using the power of words.
Most of us are where we are because of the

things we have spoken and believed about ourselves.

It is time to make a change.

I see you cause positive changes in your life and the life of your family using your words.

Your words will cause the promotion to come, it will cause the debt to be cancelled, and it will cause peace and love in your home.

Get ready for a **word activated life.**

Your words control your life.

Scriptural references: Hebrews 1:3, Proverbs 18:21

CHAPTER TWO: WORDS DETERMINE YOUR DIRECTION IN LIFE

Have you noticed how a horse is directed?

A bit is placed around the mouth of the horse.

Thus wherever the bit and the mouth moves, the horse moves too.

When the mouth of the horse is directed to the left, the horse moves to the left.

When the mouth is moved to the right, the horse moves to the right.

Thus the Bible says just like the mouth directs the horse, so does the tongue direct us.

The direction of your life today was determined by your mouth yesterday. Tomorrows' direction will be determined by your tongue today.

You had a say in where you are today.

Believe it or not, it is true.

How do you change your direction in life?

Change what you are saying about yourself and other people. Change what you are saying about your relationship.

Change what you are saying about your business.

As you change what you say, you will respond and act in the manner of your words.

That is when you will see a change in the direction of your life.

Words are powerful. They have creative power. They also have directional power.

Are your finances poor? Change what you are saying about your finances.

Instead of saying I am broke; say I am identifying several opportunities to make me millions of dollars.

Instead of saying the marriage is not working; say I receive knowledge to have the best marriage in this country.

Change what you say and you will change the direction of your life.

Scriptural Reference: JAMES 3:3-5

CHAPTER THREE: WORDS MIXED WITH FAITH WORK, NOT IDLE WORDS

Isn't it funny that most of the positive things we say, we do not believe.

Yet the negative things we say about ourselves are what we really tend to believe.

The effect is that the negative words produce harvest and the positive words are just idle.

If every word we spoke came to pass immediately, most of us will be dead by now.

Thanks to idle words, we are let go of certain words we say.

Even so, those words have a way of affecting our thinking and hence our actions.

What are idle words?

Idle words are words we just say not really believing them.

Examples:

This car is wicked. We all know cars are not wicked.

This boy will kill me. You know he won't.

When we speak a lot of idle words, it is difficult for our hearts to process which ones we believe hence our words lose potency.

That is why we must be delivered from idle and negative self-talk and so that we begin to walk in the realm of words that work and produce results.

What are faith-filled words?

They are words we speak out of the measure of

the faith of God within us.

They are words we speak without doubt.

They are words we speak having the full assurance that it is so.

It is with this confidence that Jesus tells a tree to die and it dies.

He tells the wind to be still and it is still.

Everything has ears?

Everything has ears. Whether trees, money, the wind, sickness and what have you.

That is why they respond to faith filled words.

If I were you I would begin to use my words wisely, the walls of your house might be hearing.

Ask the walls of Jericho.

Trees listened to Jesus, rains listened to Elijah, and sicknesses responded to Paul, you can be part of that list.

The list of people who speak for things to happen.

CHAPTER FOUR: KNOW WHO YOU ARE TO BE FREE FROM NEGATIVE SELF TALK

If you know who you are and who God has made you, you will not speak negatively about yourself.

I used to use a lot of negative words on myself.

Nowadays, I cannot even do that even if I want to.

This is because I know I am blessed.

I know I am the child of God. I know I do not fail.

I know I am more than a conqueror.

For these reasons, I do not even remember the last time I said anything negative about myself or anything that concerns me.

I am free from negative self-talk because I am conscious of who I am.

I have repeatedly told myself I am blessed to the extent that it has become a part of me.

I know who I am now.

Who are you?

Once you get your identity sorted out, your words will follow.

CHAPTER FIVE: SPEAK A NEW LANGUAGE

You have a new language; it is the language of faith.

Speak to everything around you.

As long as you are speaking in faith, they will hear you.

I see many changes in your life because you dared to use the power of faith filled words.

Today marks the end of negative self-talk in your life.

You will get what you say from today.

You are blessed. Keep speaking.

Speak your future today and you will see it.

I can hear you say I build houses free for people

I can hear you say I heal the sick and raise the dead.

I can hear you say my business is the number one in the world. Faith-filled words work. Do not sit idle. Speak.

MY OTHER BOOKS
Other Breakthrough Producing Books:

1. How To Have Outrageous Financial Abundance In No Time: Biblical Principles For Immediate And Overwhelming Financial Success

2. 5 Bible Promises, Prayers And Decrees That Will Give You The Best Year Ever: A Book For Shaping Every Year Successfully Plus Devotional (Book Of Promises 1)

3. Influencing The Unseen Realm: How To Influence The Spirit Realm For Victory In The Physical Realm(Spiritual Success Books)

4. Prayer That Works: Taking Responsibility For Answered Prayer

5. Healing The Sick In Five Minutes: How Anyone Can Heal Any Sickness

6. The Financial Miracle Prayer

7. The Best Secret To Answered Prayer

8. The Believer's Authority(Authority Of The Believer,Power And Authority Of The Believer)

9. The Healing Miracle Prayer

10. I Shall Not Die: Secrets To Long Life And Overcoming The Fear Of Death

11. Three Straightforward Steps To Outrageous Financial Abundance: Personal Finance (Finance Made Easy Book 1)

12. Prayers For Financial Miracles: And 3 Ways To Receive Answers Quickly

13. Book: 3 Point Blueprint For Building Strong Faith: Spiritual:Religious:Christian:Motivational

14. How To Stop Sinning Effortlessly

15. The Power Of Faith-Filled Words

16. All Sin Is Paid For: An Eye Opening Book

17. Be Happy Now:No More Depression

18. The Ultimate Christian: How To Win In Every Life Situation: A Book Full Of Revelations

19. How To Be Free From Sicknesses And Diseases(Divine Health): Divine Health Scriptures

20. Multiply Your Personal Income In Less Than 30 Days

21. Ultimate Method To Memorize The Bible Quickly: (How To Learn Scripture Memorization)

22. Overcoming Emotional Abuse

23. Passing Exams The Easy Way: 90% And Above In Exams (Learning Simplified)

24. Goal Setting For Those In A Hurry To Achieve Fast

25. Do Something Lest You Do Nothing

26. Financial Freedom:My Personal Blue-Print Made Easy For Men And Women

27. Why Men Go To Hell

28. Budgeting Tools And How My Budget Makes Me More Money

29. How To Raise Capital In 72 Hours: Quickly And Effectively Raise Capital Easily In Unconventional Ways (Finance Made Easy)

30. How To Love Unconditionally

31. Financial Independence: The Simple Path I Used To Wealth

32. Finding Happiness: The Story Of John Miller: A Christian Fiction

GET 4 POWERFUL FREE BOOKS
Click Here To Get the Books Below in Your Email

Click Here to Get them Now

Send a mail to drfrancisjonah@gmail.com for your copy

The Four Powerful Books are:
1. **All Things Are Possible**
2. **Power of I Am**
3. **Power of Praise**
4. **Power of Positive thinking**

[Click Here to Get them Now](#)

Send a mail to drfrancisjonah@gmail.com for your copy

Made in the USA
Coppell, TX
07 July 2020